Usborne Activities

General Knowledge Trivia Questions

Sam Smith and Simon Tudhope

Illustrated by Sarah Horne

Designed by Kate Rimmer

Edited by Sam Taplin

1

(1) What are the three types of medals given out at the Olympic Games?

(2) In the book by Roald Dahl, which disgusting food did the BFG eat: human beans **or** snozzcumbers?

(3) Are most London taxis...
a) yellow?   b) black?   c) red?

(4) Where are the Pyramids of Giza?
a) Saudi Arabia   b) Pakistan   c) Egypt

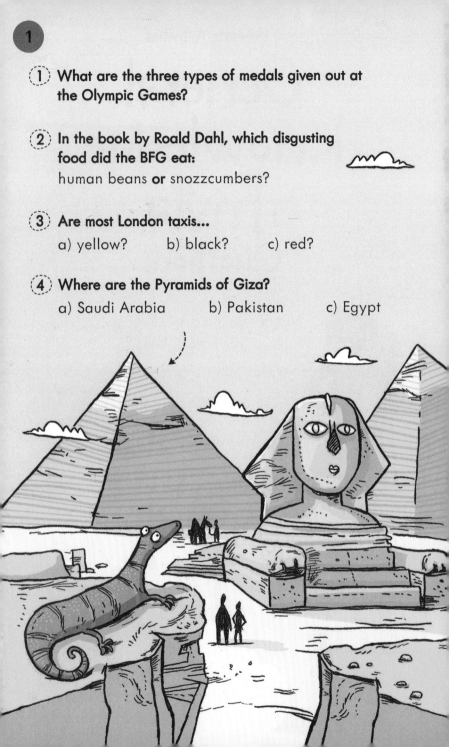

5. **In a storm, which comes first:** thunder **or** lightning?

6. **Who travels in a plane called Air Force One?**
   a) the Pope
   b) the U.S. president
   c) the queen of England

7. **Which country has the most wolves?**
   a) Canada
   b) Russia
   c) United States

8. **How many chambers does your heart have?**
   a) two   b) three   c) four

9. **The Hundred Years' War was 100 years long.**
   True or false?

AWOOOO

2

1. Which word is used for a family of lions?
   a) a boast
   b) a pride
   c) an arrogance

2. Are water molecules closer together in: ice **or** steam?

3. What scientific discovery was supposedly inspired by an apple falling from a tree?
   a) magnetism
   b) evolution
   c) gravity

4. 'Hakuna matata' is a Swahili phrase used in the movie *The Lion King*. What does it mean?
   a) no worries
   b) pardon me
   c) I'll be back

5. Complete the name of the animal that pretends to be dead, and inspired the phrase:
   'playing p _ _ _ _ m'

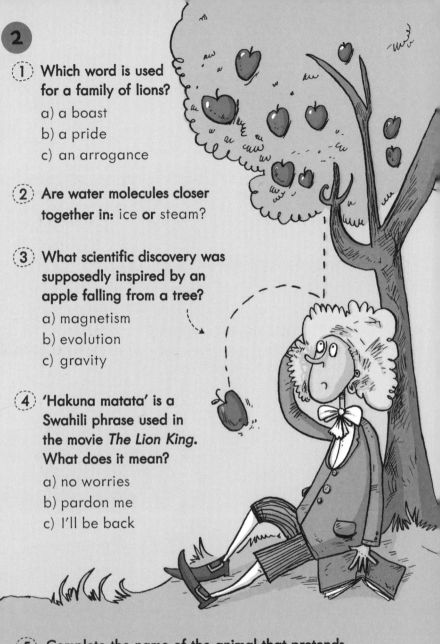

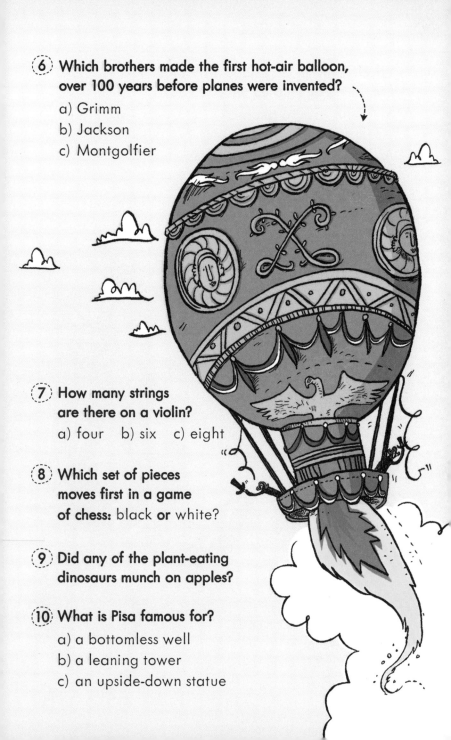

6 Which brothers made the first hot-air balloon, over 100 years before planes were invented?
a) Grimm
b) Jackson
c) Montgolfier

7 How many strings are there on a violin?
a) four   b) six   c) eight

8 Which set of pieces moves first in a game of chess: black **or** white?

9 Did any of the plant-eating dinosaurs munch on apples?

10 What is Pisa famous for?
a) a bottomless well
b) a leaning tower
c) an upside-down statue

1. **Which mythical king made a wish that meant everything he touched turned to gold?**

   a) Creon   b) Midas   c) Goldemar

2. **Are shooting stars actually stars?**

3. **I turn red at dawn and dusk, and weigh four million tons. One of my names is 'Uluru'.**

   What's my other name?

4. **Which country is home of the didgeridoo?**

   a) Australia

   b) Kenya

   c) Brazil

(5) I was a black man in a country ruled by whites.
I served 27 years in prison for fighting against racism.
I became my country's president after I was released.

Who am I?

(6) **Which sport is played at Wimbledon?**
a) golf   b) tennis   c) basketball

(7) **What is a baby kangaroo called?**
a) a billy
b) a joey
c) a sheila

(8) **In a book by C.S. Lewis, where did four children find an entrance to Narnia?**
a) in a hidden cave
b) down a rabbit hole
c) at the back of a wardrobe

(9) **What is the name for the distance from the middle of a circle to its edge?**
a) radius
b) diameter
c) circumference

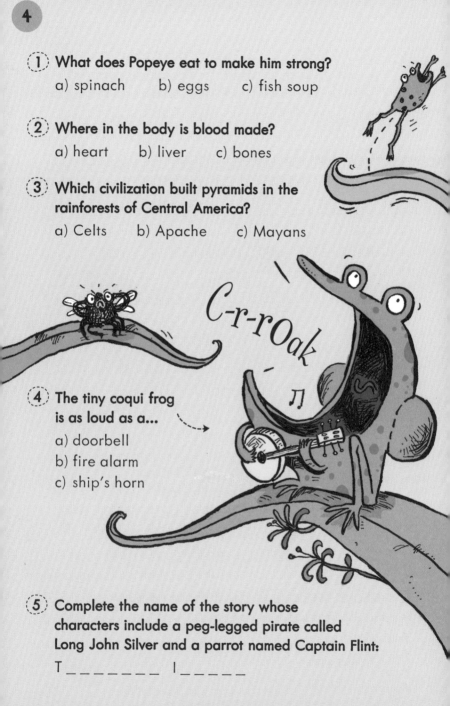

1. **What does Popeye eat to make him strong?**
   a) spinach   b) eggs   c) fish soup

2. **Where in the body is blood made?**
   a) heart   b) liver   c) bones

3. **Which civilization built pyramids in the rainforests of Central America?**
   a) Celts   b) Apache   c) Mayans

C-r-rOak

4. **The tiny coqui frog is as loud as a...**
   a) doorbell
   b) fire alarm
   c) ship's horn

5. **Complete the name of the story whose characters include a peg-legged pirate called Long John Silver and a parrot named Captain Flint:**
   T _ _ _ _ _ _ _ _   I _ _ _ _ _

6 What's the name for an acrobat's swing?

a) tightrope   b) trampoline   c) trapeze

7 The deepest part of the world's oceans is the Challenger Deep in the Mariana Trench. Roughly how deep is it?

a) 3,600ft. (1,097.3m)
b) 36,000ft. (10,973m)
c) 360,000ft. (109,730m)

8 White dwarf and red giant are both types of what?

a) galaxies   b) stars   c) planets

9 According to legend, who killed a dragon: Sir Lancelot **or** St. George?

10 An African giant snail would cover your entire...

a) face
b) chest
c) body

1. In the story of the hare and the tortoise, why did the hare lose the race?
   a) he had a thorn stuck in his foot
   b) he stopped for a nap on the way
   c) he was late for a very important date

2. In a relay race, what is the name of the object that is passed between the runners?
   a) bar   b) baguette   c) baton

3. Where did the Pied Piper supposedly come from?
   a) Germany
   b) Russia
   c) Scotland

4. This is *Hatzegopteryx*, one of the largest pterosaurs. It had the same wingspan as a...
   a) large bat
   b) large bird
   c) small plane

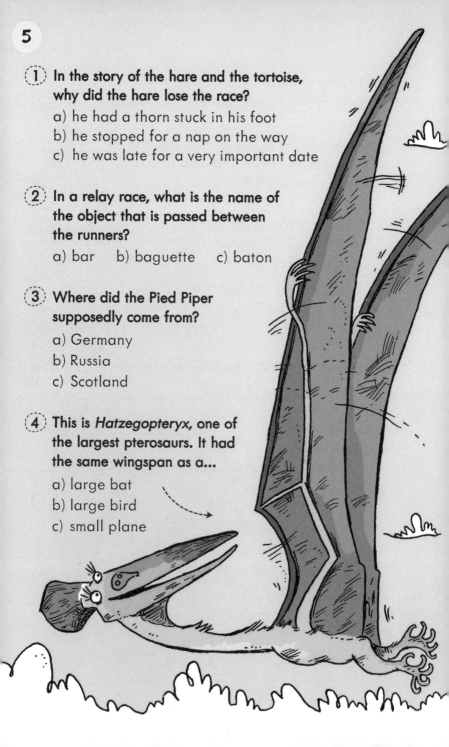

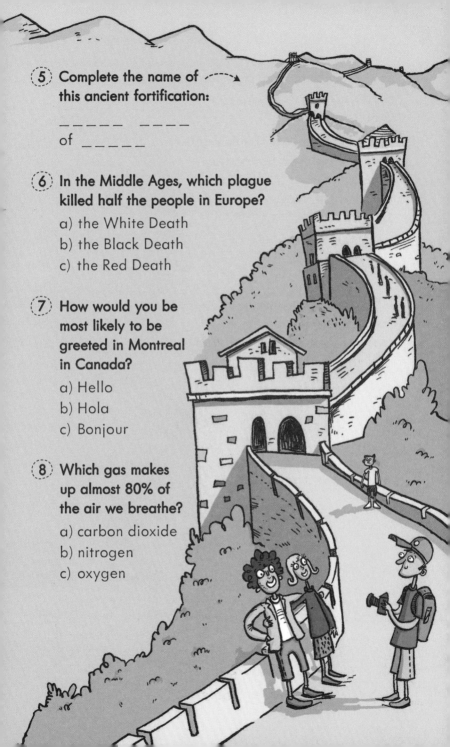

5. Complete the name of this ancient fortification:

_ _ _ _ _ _ _ _ _

of _ _ _ _ _

6. In the Middle Ages, which plague killed half the people in Europe?

a) the White Death
b) the Black Death
c) the Red Death

7. How would you be most likely to be greeted in Montreal in Canada?

a) Hello
b) Hola
c) Bonjour

8. Which gas makes up almost 80% of the air we breathe?

a) carbon dioxide
b) nitrogen
c) oxygen

(1) **Which fictional, furry creature stole Christmas:** the Grinch **or** the Grump?

(2) **What's the name of the little rolls of rice mixed with seafood or vegetables that you can eat at Japanese restaurants?**
a) gnocchi
b) ravioli
c) sushi

(3) **Who was imprisoned by the Pope for suggesting that the Earth moved around the Sun?**
a) Leonardo da Vinci
b) Galileo Galilei
c) Edwin Hubble

(4) **Slow worms are slower than earthworms.** True or false?

(5) **Which giant planet is famous for its Great Red Spot?**
   a) Jupiter   b) Uranus   c) Saturn

(6) **I can turn my head nearly all the way around. I see ten times better than humans at night. I fly in almost total silence.**

   What am I?

(7) **Diamonds are made from highly compressed...**
   a) sand   b) crystals   c) coal

(8) **How high is a standard basketball hoop?**
   a) 8ft. (2.44m)
   b) 10ft. (3.05m)
   c) 12ft. (3.66m)

(9) **What flag do pirates fly:** the Cat o' Nine Tails **or** the Jolly Roger?

(10) **In Greek mythology, Icarus flew with wings made by his dad. Why did he plummet to his death?**
   a) the sun melted the wax holding them together
   b) he was attacked by the king of the birds
   c) he panicked when he looked down

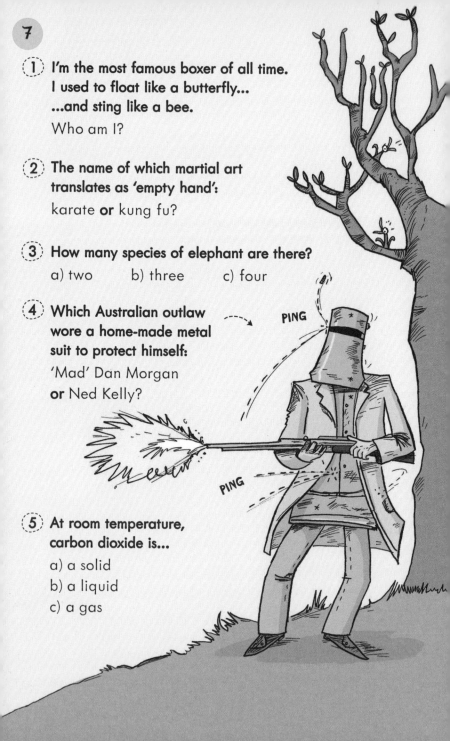

1. I'm the most famous boxer of all time.
   I used to float like a butterfly...
   ...and sting like a bee.
   Who am I?

2. The name of which martial art
   translates as 'empty hand':
   karate **or** kung fu?

3. How many species of elephant are there?
   a) two   b) three   c) four

4. Which Australian outlaw
   wore a home-made metal
   suit to protect himself:
   'Mad' Dan Morgan
   or Ned Kelly?

5. At room temperature,
   carbon dioxide is...
   a) a solid
   b) a liquid
   c) a gas

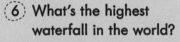

6 What's the highest
waterfall in the world?
a) Angel Falls
b) Demon Falls
c) Ghost Falls

7 Who stole the three
bears' porridge?
a) Little Miss Muffet
b) Snow White
c) Goldilocks

8 Nimbus, cirrus, cumulus
and stratus are all types
of what?
a) clouds
b) broomsticks
c) lightning

1) **What's the name of this star constellation?**
   a) Xena the Warrior
   b) Orion the Hunter
   c) Brian the Blacksmith

2) **Who was the first president of the United States?**
   a) Barack Obama
   b) Ronald Reagan
   c) George Washington

3) **If you poured a cup of oil into a cup of water, what would happen?**
   a) the oil would float on the surface
   b) the oil would mix with the water
   c) the oil would sink to the bottom

4) **Roughly how long were the dinosaurs around for?**
   a) 65 million years
   b) 165 million years
   c) 265 million years

5 Match each tawny owl with its call:

   a) male   1) tu-whit

   b) female   2) tu-whoo

Tu-Whit

6 One fifth of all the people in the world are Chinese. True or false?

Tu-whOOoo

7 A 'boneshaker' was an early form of what?

   a) bicycle   b) car   c) dentist's drill

8 Can a rattlesnake hear its own rattle?

9 In the story by Julia Donaldson, which terrifying beast did the mouse tell the other animals he was going to eat with:

the Gruffalo **or** the Jabberwock?

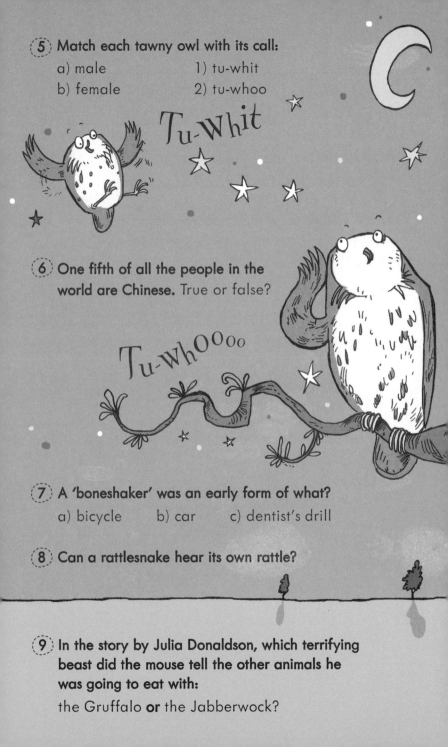

1) In the *Harry Potter* books, how was baby Harry delivered to his aunt and uncle's house?

a) broomstick   b) flying carpet   c) flying motorcycle

2) Which side of a ship is starboard:
left **or** right?

3) In the fight for the English throne called the Wars of the Roses, the heraldic roses of the two sides were...

a) yellow and blue
b) red and white
c) black and white

4) What are a meerkat's greatest enemies?

a) snakes
b) jackals
c) birds of prey

5 In which sport would a Fosbury Flop be performed?

   a) diving   b) high jump   c) wrestling

6 Which character has a blue box that can travel through time and space?

   a) Doctor Who
   b) Captain Kirk
   c) Darth Vader

7 Where is St. Basil's cathedral?

   a) Finland
   b) Russia
   c) Scotland

8 How many bacteria live in your body?

   a) none
   b) 10 million
   c) 100 trillion

9 What is a group of crows called: a funeral **or** a murder?

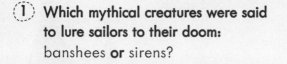

1. Which mythical creatures were said to lure sailors to their doom: banshees **or** sirens?

2. In 1929, which American gangster ordered the St. Valentine's Day Massacre?
   a) Al Capone
   b) Bugsy Malone
   c) Vito Corleone

3. I was a giant, once said to hold the world on my shoulders. I gave my name to a mountain range and a book full of maps. Who am I?

4. What were dinosaurs?
   a) amphibians   b) reptiles   c) mammals

5. Who were the Three Musketeers? Athos, Porthos and...
   a) d'Artagnan   b) Aramis   c) Richelieu

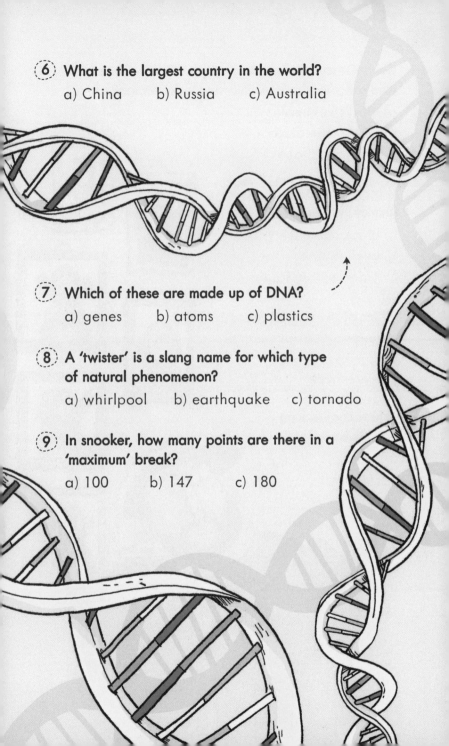

6) **What is the largest country in the world?**
   a) China   b) Russia   c) Australia

7) **Which of these are made up of DNA?**
   a) genes   b) atoms   c) plastics

8) **A 'twister' is a slang name for which type of natural phenomenon?**
   a) whirlpool   b) earthquake   c) tornado

9) **In snooker, how many points are there in a 'maximum' break?**
   a) 100   b) 147   c) 180

1) Count Dracula is based on which historic prince, who executed his enemies on wooden stakes?
   a) Vlad the Impaler
   b) Grisha the Gorer
   c) Bram the Staker

2) What's the most venomous animal in the world?
   a) black mamba
   b) box jellyfish
   c) black widow spider

3) 'Ships of the desert' are...
   a) jeeps
   b) camels
   c) hovercraft

4) Which English king had six wives?
   a) Charles I
   b) Richard III
   c) Henry VIII

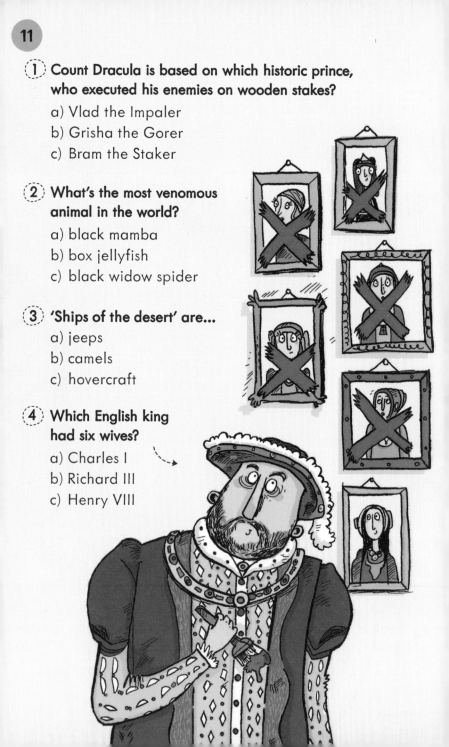

5) **What is a material that doesn't conduct electricity called:** a resistor **or** an insulator?

6) **Which cartoon character thought he saw a pussycat?**
a) Goofy   b) Jerry   c) Tweety Pie

7) **If a sailor was left stranded on a desert island, they would say they had been what?**
a) marooned   b) capsized   c) scuppered

8) **What does the Latin name** *Tyrannosaurus rex* **mean?**
a) giant royal lizard
b) prince of the meat-eaters
c) tyrant lizard king

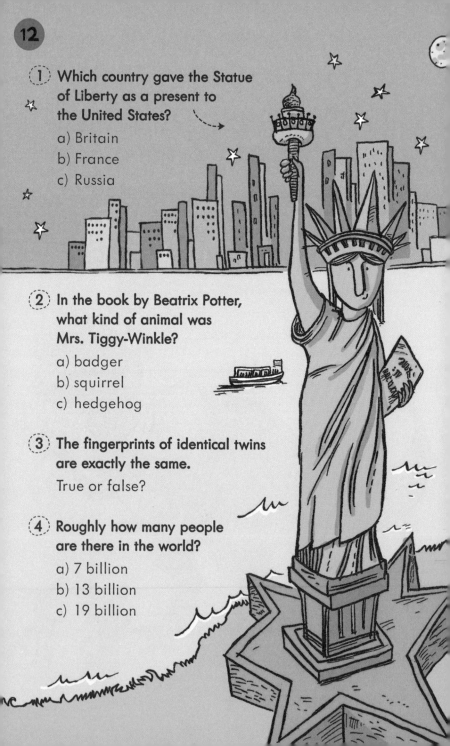

1. Which country gave the Statue of Liberty as a present to the United States?
   a) Britain
   b) France
   c) Russia

2. In the book by Beatrix Potter, what kind of animal was Mrs. Tiggy-Winkle?
   a) badger
   b) squirrel
   c) hedgehog

3. The fingerprints of identical twins are exactly the same.
   True or false?

4. Roughly how many people are there in the world?
   a) 7 billion
   b) 13 billion
   c) 19 billion

5 If a flea were the size of a human, its leap would be the equivalent of jumping...

a) over a bus
b) over a skyscraper
c) over a mountain

6 Which flowers is Vincent van Gogh most famous for painting: sunflowers **or** water lilies?

7 I was a fearsome horseback warrior from Mongolia, and the most successful conqueror of all time. One of my grandsons was Kublai Khan.

Who am I?

8 According to the nursery rhyme, Tuesday's child...

a) has far to go
b) is full of grace
c) is loving and giving

1. **Which material is magnetic?**
   a) steel   b) wood   c) plastic

2. **Where would you find manga?**
   a) in a circus
   b) in a fruit market
   c) in a comic book store

3. **Which camera picks up people's body heat, so they can be seen in the dark?**
   a) ultraviolet camera
   b) high-definition camera
   c) infrared camera

4. **In the Middle Ages, which animals were often used by doctors:**
   slugs **or** leeches?

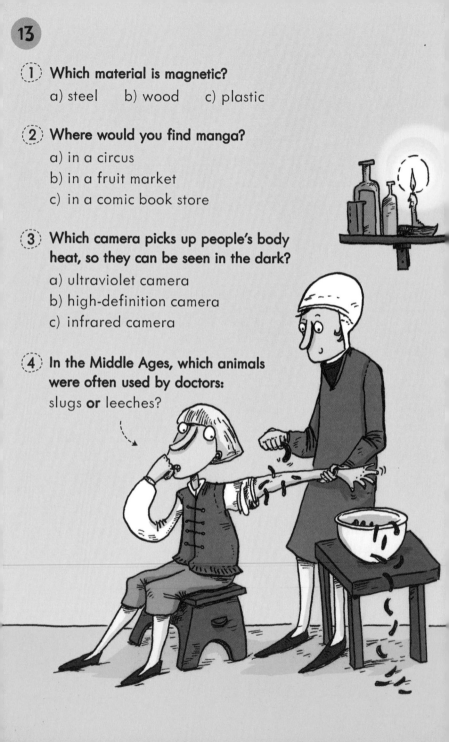

5 In Rudyard Kipling's *Just So Stories,* how did the Elephant's Child get his trunk?

   a) his nose grew every time he told a lie

   b) his nose got stretched by a crocodile

   c) he drank from an enchanted waterhole

6 What is the capital city of Australia?

   a) Canberra

   b) Melbourne

   c) Sydney

7 What was the first and only passenger plane to break the sound barrier?

   a) Airbus A330

   b) Boeing 747

   c) Concorde

8 Who defeated Napoleon at the Battle of Waterloo?

   a) Lord Nelson

   b) Sir Francis Drake

   c) Duke of Wellington

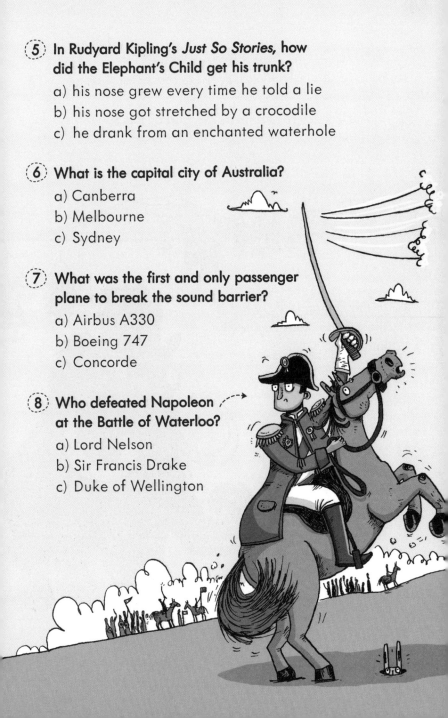

1) **Who fell in love with a robot called EVE?**
   a) C-3PO   b) WALL-E   c) Inspector Gadget

2) **In Ancient Egypt, who was the god of the Sun?**
   a) Anubis   b) Osiris   c) Ra

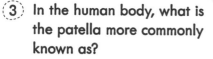

3) **In the human body, what is the patella more commonly known as?**
   a) jawbone
   b) kneecap
   c) shoulder blade

4) **Did cavemen ever hunt woolly mammoths?**

5) **Where is the London home of the British Prime Minister?**
   a) 10 Downing Street
   b) Buckingham Palace
   c) Houses of Parliament

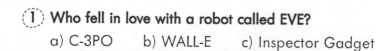

6) In 1912, why did the first woman to fly across the English Channel get so little attention from the media?

a) it was frowned upon for women to fly
b) the *Titanic* had sunk the day before
c) no one believed her

7) What is it called when the Moon temporarily blocks the light from the Sun?

S _ _ _ _   e _ _ _ _ _ _

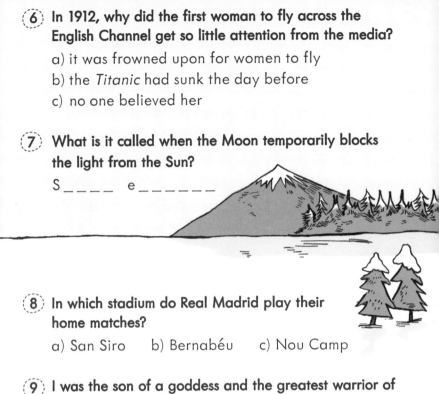

8) In which stadium do Real Madrid play their home matches?

a) San Siro   b) Bernabéu   c) Nou Camp

9) I was the son of a goddess and the greatest warrior of the Trojan War. My only weak spot was my heel.

Who am I?

10) Which animal causes more human deaths than any other on the planet?

a) tiger   b) crocodile   c) mosquito

11) In *Star Trek*, which of these statements would you associate with Mr. Spock?

a) "Beam me up, Scotty."
b) "Resistance is futile."
c) "Live long and prosper."

1. **What belt are karate experts entitled to wear?**
   a) white belt   b) red belt   c) black belt

2. **Who was the architect of this strange church in Barcelona which is still being built today:**
   Pablo Picasso **or** Antoni Gaudí?

3. **Which expensive food is made entirely of fish eggs?**
   a) borscht
   b) caviar
   c) blini

4. **I live on an island near Australia, and I have extremely strong jaws. My cartoon character spins like a tornado.**
   What am I?

5. **What's the capital city of Greece?**
   a) Athens
   b) Olympus
   c) Troy

6 What process do plants use to turn the Sun's energy into food?
   a) metamorphosis
   b) photosynthesis
   c) hypnosis

7 Who invented the World Wide Web?
   a) Tim Berners-Lee
   b) Bill Gates
   c) Charles Babbage

8 Match the animal to its description:
   a) tiger   1) herbivore
   b) bear   2) carnivore
   c) sheep   3) omnivore

1. **Where would you find the Sea of Tranquility and the Ocean of Storms?**
   a) underneath the Antarctic ice sheet
   b) off the Horn of Africa
   c) on the Moon

2. **DNA is an acid.** True or false?

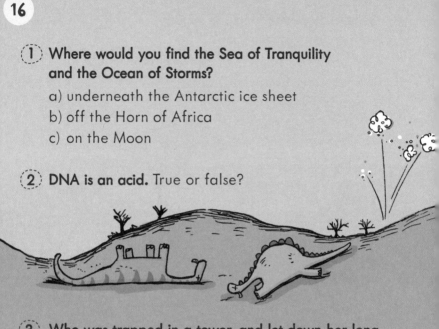

3. **Who was trapped in a tower, and let down her long, golden hair for a prince to climb up?**
   a) Cinderella   b) Snow White   c) Rapunzel

4. **Which animal completes these lines by William Blake?**
   'T _ _ _ _ _, T _ _ _ _ burning bright,
   In the forests of the night.'

5. **What are the three disciplines in a modern triathlon?**
   a) skating, skiing and shooting
   b) running, swimming and cycling
   c) high jump, long jump and triple jump

6. **For how long was Lady Jane Grey queen of England:**
   nine days **or** nine years?

7. **How is the shelled, green foursome of Leonardo, Donatello, Raphael and Michelangelo better known?**

8. Which tree grows from an acorn?
   a) horse chestnut   b) oak   c) willow

9. Who was the first person to reach the South Pole:
   Roald Amundsen **or** Roald Dahl?

10. During which period did the dinosaurs become extinct?
    a) Cretaceous
    b) Jurassic
    c) Triassic

1. In *The Hunger Games,* what is Katniss Everdeen's weapon of choice?
   a) bow and arrow
   b) straight sword
   c) catapult

2. How was Queen Marie Antoinette executed during the French Revolution?
   a) trebuchet
   b) guillotine
   c) bagatelle

3. Which river flows through the middle of Paris?
   a) Rhine
   b) Seine
   c) Danube

4. Which planet's surface temperature is the hottest: Mercury **or** Venus?

5 Who holds the record for winning the most Formula One driving championships?

a) Ayrton Senna
b) Lewis Hamilton
c) Michael Schumacher

6 I'm a plumber with a red cap. I rescue Princess Peach from the evil Bowser.

Who am I?

7 Which of these was NOT a real outlaw?

a) The Lone Ranger
b) Billy the Kid
c) The Sundance Kid

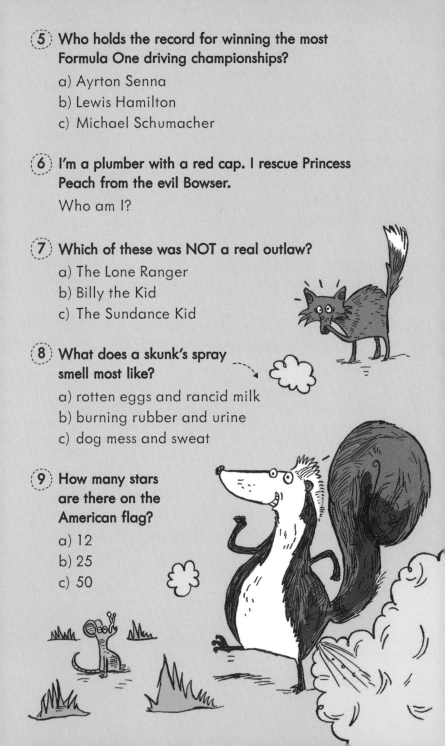

8 What does a skunk's spray smell most like?

a) rotten eggs and rancid milk
b) burning rubber and urine
c) dog mess and sweat

9 How many stars are there on the American flag?

a) 12
b) 25
c) 50

1. **Which country has the longest coastline?**
   a) Australia   b) Canada   c) Russia

2. **Teddy bears were named after the U.S. president Theodore Roosevelt.** True or false?

3. **A cannonball and a tennis ball are dropped from the top of a tower at the same time. What happens next?**
   a) the cannonball hits the ground first
   b) the tennis ball hits the ground first
   c) both balls hit the ground at the same time

4. **Which Roman emperor was said to have played his fiddle while the city of Rome burned?**
   a) Tiberius   b) Caligula   c) Nero

5. **In *The Hobbit* by J.R.R. Tolkien, what does Gollum think Bilbo Baggins stole from him?**
   a) a sword   b) a ring   c) a jewel

6. **There is a frog that makes its own claws by breaking the bones in its wrist and forcing them through its skin. Find the letter that fills all the gaps in its name:**
   ho _ _ o _ frog

7. **Flamingo chicks are pink.**
   True or false?

8 I was the largest and most luxurious ship ever built. They called me 'unsinkable'... but I hit an iceberg in the Atlantic and sank on my first voyage.
What am I?

9 Which type of race is named after an ancient battle?

   a) steeplechase
   b) cross-country
   c) marathon

10 These ancient statues are on which island in the Pacific Ocean?

   a) Christmas Island
   b) Easter Island
   c) Valentine Island

1 **What does the name 'archosaur' mean?**
   a) first lizard
   b) ruling lizard
   c) ancestor lizard

2 **Who "went to sea in a beautiful pea-green boat"?**
   a) Bobby Shafto
   b) Sinbad the Sailor
   c) The Owl and the Pussycat

3 **The Treaty of Versailles marked the end of which war?**
   a) First World War
   b) Second World War
   c) Gulf War

4 **In India, which type of snake would a snake charmer be most likely to use?**
   a) cobra
   b) mamba
   c) viper

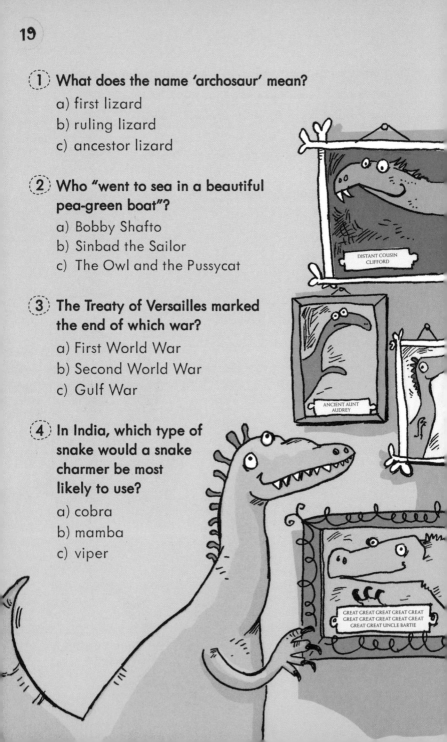

DISTANT COUSIN CLIFFORD

ANCIENT AUNT AUDREY

GREAT GREAT GREAT GREAT GREAT GREAT GREAT GREAT GREAT GREAT GREAT GREAT UNCLE BARTIE

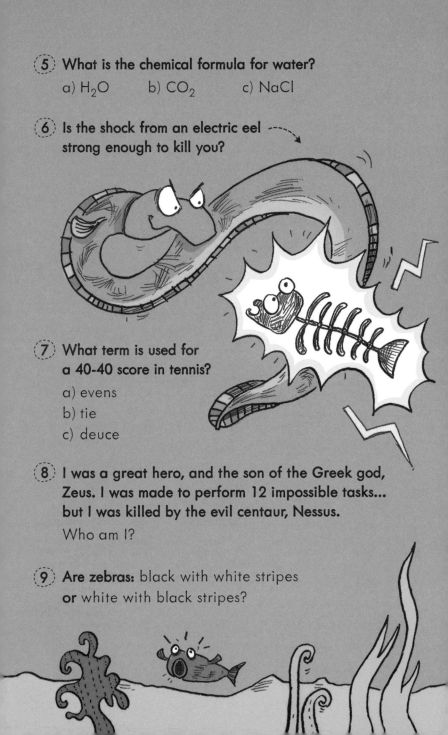

(5) What is the chemical formula for water?

a) H_2O b) CO_2 c) NaCl

(6) Is the shock from an electric eel strong enough to kill you?

(7) What term is used for a 40-40 score in tennis?

a) evens
b) tie
c) deuce

(8) I was a great hero, and the son of the Greek god, Zeus. I was made to perform 12 impossible tasks... but I was killed by the evil centaur, Nessus.

Who am I?

(9) **Are zebras:** black with white stripes **or** white with black stripes?

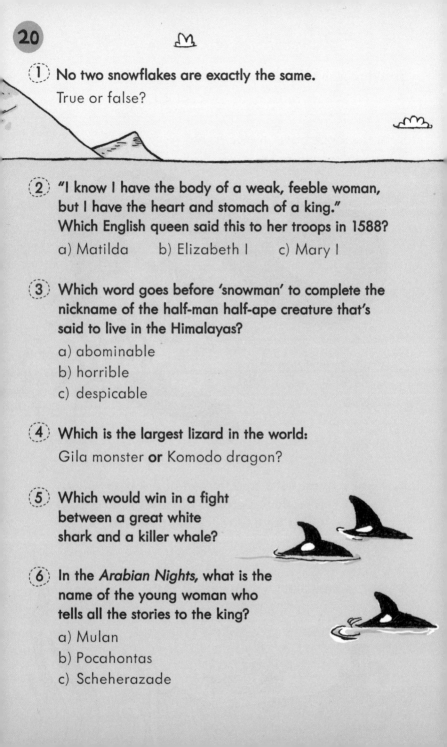

1) No two snowflakes are exactly the same.
True or false?

2) "I know I have the body of a weak, feeble woman, but I have the heart and stomach of a king." Which English queen said this to her troops in 1588?
a) Matilda   b) Elizabeth I   c) Mary I

3) Which word goes before 'snowman' to complete the nickname of the half-man half-ape creature that's said to live in the Himalayas?
a) abominable
b) horrible
c) despicable

4) Which is the largest lizard in the world:
Gila monster **or** Komodo dragon?

5) Which would win in a fight between a great white shark and a killer whale?

6) In the *Arabian Nights,* what is the name of the young woman who tells all the stories to the king?
a) Mulan
b) Pocahontas
c) Scheherazade

(7) Who led the first expedition to sail around the world, but died on the way:

Ferdinand Magellan **or** Christopher Columbus?

(8) What is the name of the vehicle that Scooby Doo and his gang travel around in?

a) The Turbo Terrific
b) The Mystery Machine
c) Chitty Chitty Bang Bang

(9) Roughly how many times does your heart usually beat in one minute?

a) 20   b) 80   c) 140

(10) What was New York originally called?

a) New Paris   b) New London   c) New Amsterdam

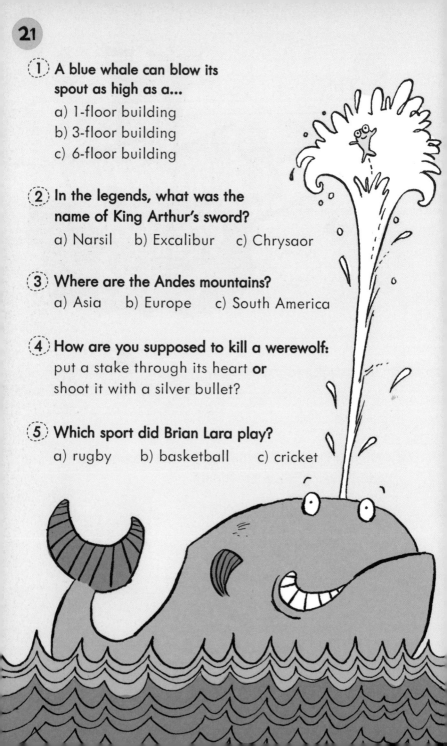

1. **A blue whale can blow its spout as high as a...**
   a) 1-floor building
   b) 3-floor building
   c) 6-floor building

2. **In the legends, what was the name of King Arthur's sword?**
   a) Narsil   b) Excalibur   c) Chrysaor

3. **Where are the Andes mountains?**
   a) Asia   b) Europe   c) South America

4. **How are you supposed to kill a werewolf:** put a stake through its heart **or** shoot it with a silver bullet?

5. **Which sport did Brian Lara play?**
   a) rugby   b) basketball   c) cricket

6 Who was the first person in space?
a) Neil Armstrong
b) Yuri Gagarin
c) James T. Kirk

7 Eskimos have over 50 words for snow. True or false?

8 My boss is M.
My colleague is Q.
My codename is 007.

Who am I?

BOCTOK 1

9 Which singer made the 'moonwalk' famous?
a) Michael Jackson   b) Madonna   c) Beyoncé

10 What is Spain's capital city?
a) Madrid   b) Seville   c) Barcelona

1. If you say someone has blue eyes, which part of their eyes are you describing?

   a) cornea   b) iris   c) pupil

2. What's the name of the space marine in *Toy Story*?

   a) Stan Starman
   b) Rocket Tex
   c) Buzz Lightyear

3. Put these civilizations in time order, oldest first:

   a) Aztec   b) Spartan   c) Byzantine

4. I was born from the death of a massive star. I grow by sucking in everything around me. Nothing can escape, not even light.

   What am I?

5. If all your blood vessels were laid out end to end, how far would they stretch?

   a) twice around a football field
   b) twice around New York City
   c) twice around the Equator

6. What is the mythical bird that dies in a ball of flames and is then reborn from the ashes?

   a) phoenix   b) thunderbird   c) dodo

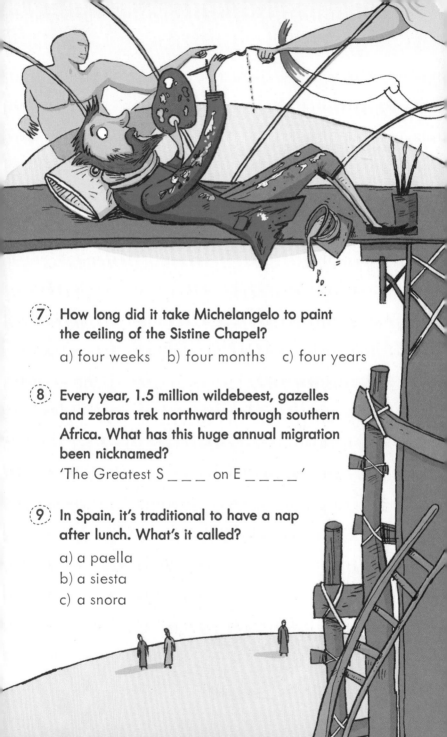

7 How long did it take Michelangelo to paint the ceiling of the Sistine Chapel?

a) four weeks   b) four months   c) four years

8 Every year, 1.5 million wildebeest, gazelles and zebras trek northward through southern Africa. What has this huge annual migration been nicknamed?

'The Greatest S _ _ _ on E _ _ _ _ _'

9 In Spain, it's traditional to have a nap after lunch. What's it called?

a) a paella

b) a siesta

c) a snora

1. In *Transformers,* who is the leader of the Autobots?
   a) Megatron   b) Sonny   c) Optimus Prime

2. Which jersey does the leading rider in the Tour de France cycle race wear?
   a) red jersey
   b) yellow jersey
   c) blue jersey

3. What's opposite to southeast?

4. What type of boat is this man paddling through the canals of Venice?

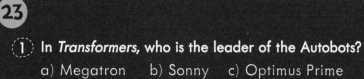

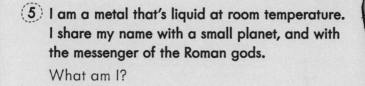

5 I am a metal that's liquid at room temperature. I share my name with a small planet, and with the messenger of the Roman gods.

What am I?

6 Which loch (lake) in Scotland is said to be home to a prehistoric sea reptile?

a) Loch Bess
b) Loch Mess
c) Loch Ness

7 What type of animal is a bat?

a) mammal
b) bird
c) reptile

8 Which storybook hero said "Please sir, I want some more."?

a) Oliver Twist
b) Tom Sawyer
c) Harry Potter

1. What legendary ghost ship is said to be condemned to sail the seven seas for all eternity?
   a) *The Dawn Treader*
   b) *The Flying Dutchman*
   c) *The Black Pearl*

2. Can a passenger plane survive being struck by lightning?

3. In 1605, who was caught trying to blow up the Houses of Parliament in London?
   a) William Wallace
   b) Guy Fawkes
   c) Wat Tyler

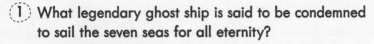

4. Which rays do doctors use to look at people's bones?
   a) X-rays
   b) gamma rays
   c) ultraviolet rays

5. In 2007, sharks killed one human. How many sharks did humans kill in the same year?
   a) 1 million   b) 10 million   c) 100 million

(6) 'Smoke that Thunders' is the translation of the local name for the world's largest:

volcano **or** waterfall?

(7) Put these golf scores in order, from best to worst:

a) bogey b) eagle c) par d) birdie

(8) What are the summer storms called that provide over 80% of India's annual rainfall?

a) monsoons b) typhoons c) hurricanes

(9) What type of scan is used to see unborn babies?

a) MRI
b) radar
c) ultrasound

1. Sailors on long voyages used to suffer from a deadly disease called scurvy. Which food could prevent it?

   a) bread   b) lemons   c) meat

2. Which of these composers went deaf?

   a) Beethoven
   b) Wagner
   c) Mozart

3. Which flag does a surrendering army wave?

   a) black flag   b) white flag   c) red flag

4. Norway is sometimes known as the land of what: the rising sun **or** the midnight sun?

5. Which of these melts ice?

   a) pepper   b) salt   c) sugar

6 A praying mantis strikes how many times faster than a person can blink?
a) 3 times
b) 10 times
c) 50 times

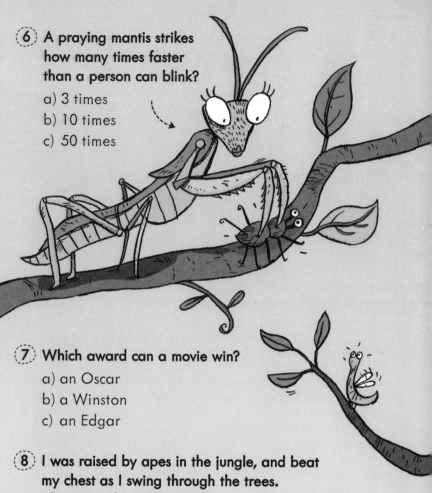

7 Which award can a movie win?
a) an Oscar
b) a Winston
c) an Edgar

8 I was raised by apes in the jungle, and beat my chest as I swing through the trees. I have a wife called Jane.

Who am I?

9 How long does it take the Earth to go around the Sun?
a) a day   b) a month   c) a year

10 When Queen Marie Antoinette was told that her people had no bread, she cruelly said: "Let them eat cake." True or false?

1. In *Frozen,* what is the name of the snowman who likes warm hugs and dreams of summer?
   a) Olaf   b) Hans   c) Sven

2. Where are the smallest bones in your body?
   a) ear   b) eye   c) nose

3. What type of artwork is made by gluing lots of pieces of paper and other items together?
   a) origami   b) etching   c) collage

4. What word completes the quotation from *E.T. the Extra-Terrestrial*?
   "E.T. p _ _ _ _ home."

5. How far away can you hear a lion's roar?
   a) 1.5km (1 mile)
   b) 8km (5 miles)
   c) 16km (10 miles)

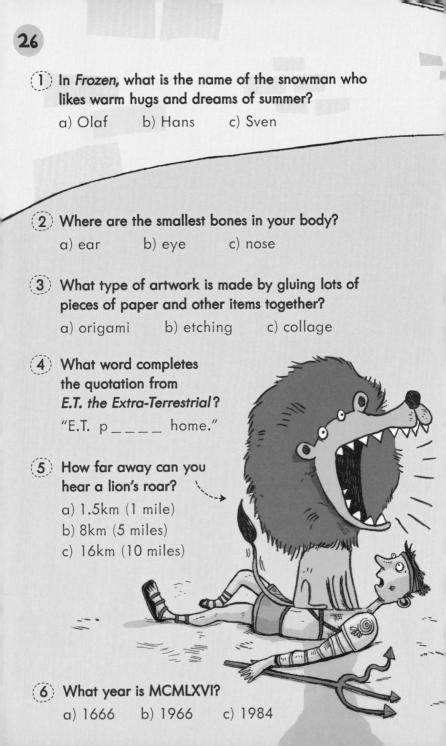

6. What year is MCMLXVI?
   a) 1666   b) 1966   c) 1984

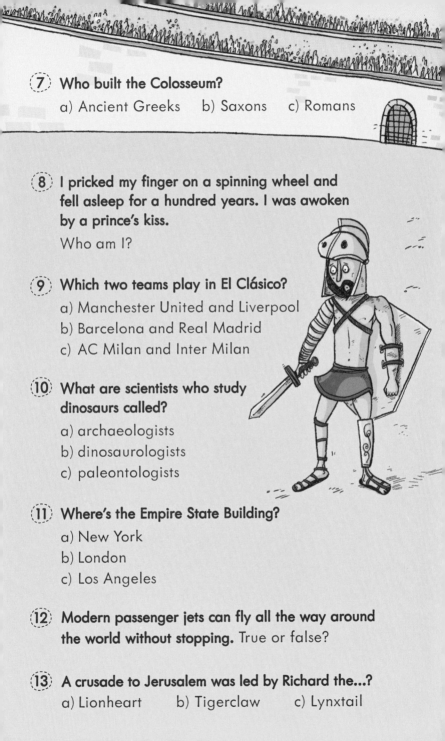

7 Who built the Colosseum?

a) Ancient Greeks   b) Saxons   c) Romans

8 I pricked my finger on a spinning wheel and fell asleep for a hundred years. I was awoken by a prince's kiss.

Who am I?

9 Which two teams play in El Clásico?

a) Manchester United and Liverpool
b) Barcelona and Real Madrid
c) AC Milan and Inter Milan

10 What are scientists who study dinosaurs called?

a) archaeologists
b) dinosaurologists
c) paleontologists

11 Where's the Empire State Building?

a) New York
b) London
c) Los Angeles

12 Modern passenger jets can fly all the way around the world without stopping. True or false?

13 A crusade to Jerusalem was led by Richard the...?

a) Lionheart   b) Tigerclaw   c) Lynxtail

1. If you traced around Italy's coastline on a map, what would your picture look like?

   a) a boot   b) a horn   c) a star

2. Traditionally, what are the two main types of plays: comedy and...?

3. Which mysterious criminal terrorized the streets of London in the 1880s?

   a) the Artful Dodger
   b) Jack the Ripper
   c) Professor Moriarty

4. What does a beaver do when it's frightened?

   a) chatters its teeth
   b) gnaws down a tree
   c) slaps the water with its tail

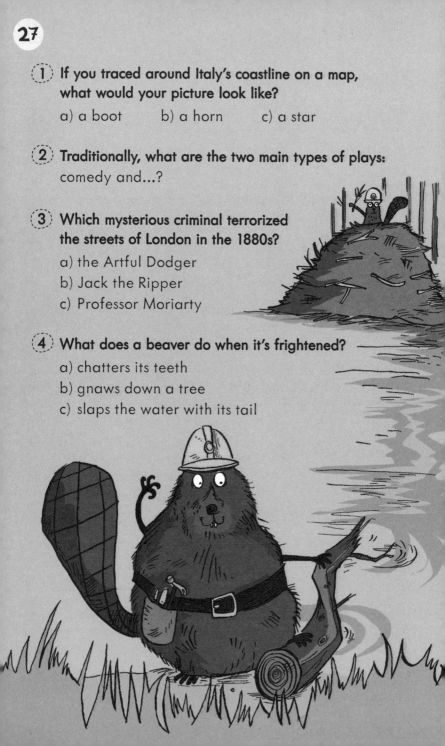

5) **Which fictional sea beast was hunted by Captain Ahab?**
   a) Moby Dick   b) Hydra   c) Leviathan

6) **How many sides does a nonagon have: none or nine?**

7) **On what day in 1776 did America declare independence from Great Britain?**
   a) February 14th   b) July 4th   c) October 31st

8) **What's the gas that makes your voice go high-pitched and squeaky when you breathe it in?**
   a) helium
   b) methane
   c) hydrogen

9) **Which fish lures its prey with a bright light?**
   a) goblin shark
   b) gulper eel
   c) angler fish

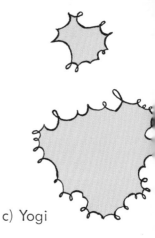

1 **What are mapmakers called?**
 a) cartographers
 b) orienteers
 c) geographers

2 **Which resident of Jellystone Park is "smarter than the average bear"?**
 a) Baloo   b) Winnie the Pooh   c) Yogi

3 **If you were stranded on a desert island, which shape should you make on the beach to attract a search plane?**
 a) triangle   b) circle   c) square

4 **What has bat dung been used to make?**
 a) gunpowder   b) cement   c) perfume

5 **Who, in the Middle Ages, experimented with potions and metals, trying to create the Philosopher's Stone and the Elixir of Life?**
 a) crusaders   b) alchemists   c) sorcerers

6 In *The Wind in the Willows,* what type of vehicle does Mr. Toad steal?

a) motorcar   b) horse-drawn caravan   c) barge

7 Which small fish from the Amazon river could bite off your finger with one snip of its razor-sharp teeth?

a) piranha   b) viper fish   c) barracuda

8 Which of these cities is NOT built on a cluster of islands?

a) New York   b) Venice   c) Madrid

9 What's the name of the creatures that Professor Oak studies, and that trainers use to fight each other?

a) tamagotchi   b) pokémon   c) digimon

10 The speedy ships that sailed between Europe and China in the mid-19th century were known as what?

a) sugar sloops
b) coffee cutters
c) tea clippers

11 Is a chemical reaction that gives out heat called:

endothermic **or** exothermic?

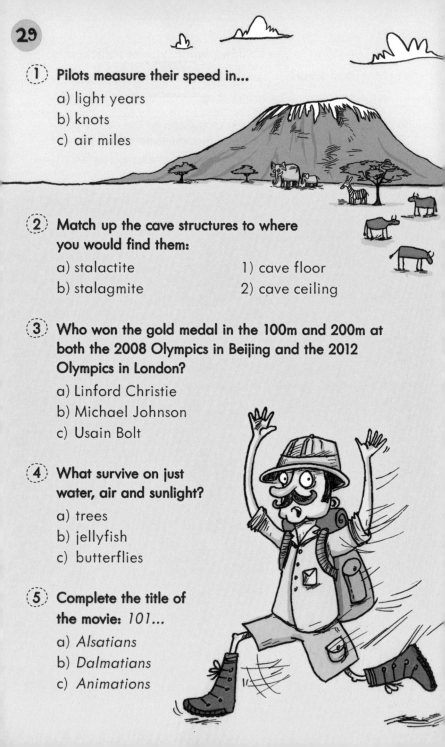

1) Pilots measure their speed in...
   a) light years
   b) knots
   c) air miles

2) Match up the cave structures to where you would find them:
   a) stalactite
   b) stalagmite
   1) cave floor
   2) cave ceiling

3) Who won the gold medal in the 100m and 200m at both the 2008 Olympics in Beijing and the 2012 Olympics in London?
   a) Linford Christie
   b) Michael Johnson
   c) Usain Bolt

4) What survive on just water, air and sunlight?
   a) trees
   b) jellyfish
   c) butterflies

5) Complete the title of the movie: *101...*
   a) *Alsatians*
   b) *Dalmatians*
   c) *Animations*

6 **What's the name of the Paris prison that was stormed by a mob in 1789 at the start of the French Revolution:** the Bastille **or** the Château d'If?

7 **The gemstones called sapphires are usually...**
   a) red   b) green   c) blue

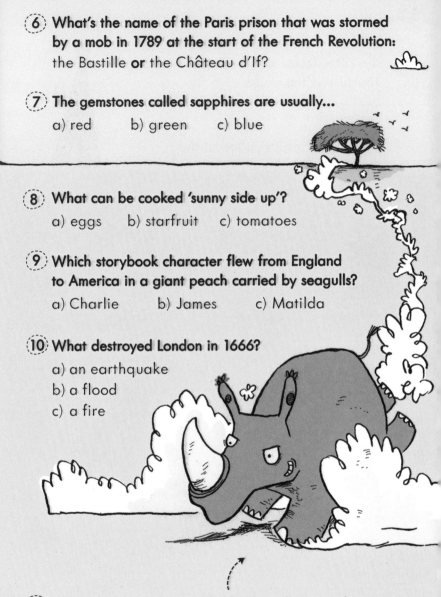

8 **What can be cooked 'sunny side up'?**
   a) eggs   b) starfruit   c) tomatoes

9 **Which storybook character flew from England to America in a giant peach carried by seagulls?**
   a) Charlie   b) James   c) Matilda

10 **What destroyed London in 1666?**
   a) an earthquake
   b) a flood
   c) a fire

11 **What's the best way to deal with a charging rhino?**
   a) stand your ground, shouting and screaming
   b) keep quiet and throw a rock to one side
   c) punch it on the nose

1. When it was completed in 1889, the Eiffel Tower was the tallest structure in the world.

   True or false?

2. Who made his last stand at the **Little Bighorn:** General Custer **or** General Patton?

3. Who is Iron Man's girlfriend?
   a) Pepper Potts
   b) Iron Lady
   c) Lois Lane

4. What is used to play ice hockey?
   a) a ball
   b) a shuttle
   c) a puck

5. Does a banana have DNA?

6. If you step west to east across the International Date Line, do you go: back one day **or** forward one day?

7. Do lemmings hurl themselves off the edges of cliffs?

8. In the middle of the Jurassic period, the Earth had two continents. One is known as Gondwana, the other is known as...
   a) Laurasia
   b) Ellafrica
   c) Annamerica

gondwana

9. In the book by Eoin Colfer, what type of creature does Artemis Fowl kidnap?
   a) troll
   b) elf
   c) centaur

10. Which of these substances is an acid?
    a) vinegar
    b) water
    c) soap

1) Which rocket took astronauts to the Moon for the first time?

a) Apollo 1   b) Apollo 11   c) Apollo 13

2) From how great a height could a mouse fall and survive?

a) the roof of a house
b) the top of a crane
c) a cruising jumbo jet

3) My friend is Doctor Watson, and my enemy is the Napoleon of crime. I live at 221b Baker Street.
Who am I?

4) Only one of the Poles has land beneath its ice. Which is it: North **or** South?

5. Which 16th-century English playwright wrote *Romeo and Juliet*?

6. **If you were cast adrift in space without a spacesuit, you would explode.** True or false?

7. **Which of these statements about lobsters is NOT true?**
   a) they scream when chefs boil them alive
   b) they can live for over a hundred years
   c) they were once fed mainly to slaves

8. **In bullfights, do matadors use...**
   a) a red cape?   b) a black cape?   c) a blue cape?

9. **In *The Muppet Show*, who is Miss Piggy in love with?**
   a) Rizzo the Rat
   b) The Great Gonzo
   c) Kermit the Frog

10. **Whose dead body has been on display in Moscow's Red Square since 1924?**
    a) Benito Mussolini
    b) Vladimir Lenin
    c) Chairman Mao

11. **What is the largest animal that's ever lived?**
    a) *Diplodocus*   b) giant squid   c) blue whale

1. **What did miners once take down the mines with them to test the safety of the air?**
   a) cats   b) rats   c) canaries

2. **Are killer whales really whales?**

3. **Where's the Taj Mahal?**
   a) India   b) China   c) Iran

4. **Roughly how much blood is there in your body?**
   a) 2 pints
   b) 8 pints
   c) 14 pints

5 How do you say 'goodbye' in Japanese?

a) konnichiwa   b) sashimi   c) sayonara

6 What did Alfred Nobel, who gives his name to the Nobel prizes, invent: dynamite **or** vaccination?

7 Who was the first cricketer to score one hundred international centuries, and has the nickname 'The Little Master'?

a) Ricky Ponting
b) Sachin Tendulkar
c) Geoffrey Boycott

8 We sailed in longships. We loved fighting and feasting. We were the scourge of northern Europe.

Who are we?

1 What did Han Solo fly in *Star Wars*?

a) Death Star   b) TIE fighter   c) *Millennium Falcon*

2 Where is it rude to finish all the food on your plate because it indicates that you weren't given enough to eat?

a) China   b) France   c) Brazil

3 In which sport can you take part in a scrum, smash into other players, and score a try?

a) ice hockey   b) rugby   c) American football

4 What was the name of the sheep that was the first ever cloned mammal?

a) Dolly   b) Molly   c) Polly

5. **Who painted the *Mona Lisa*?**
   a) Pablo Picasso
   b) Auguste Renoir
   c) Leonardo da Vinci

6. **Cows always lie down when it's raining.**
   True or false?

7. **In the poem by Dr. Seuss, what dish does Sam-I-Am want to serve?**
   a) a rack of lamb
   b) green eggs and ham
   c) brown bread and jam

8. **Why do bees dance?**
   a) to attract a mate
   b) to avoid predators
   c) to signal where food is

9. **In the very first Olympic Games, which of these was NOT one of the events?**
   a) archery
   b) naked wrestling
   c) a race in full battle dress

1. **Roughly how long does it take light from the Sun to reach the Earth?**
   a) eight milliseconds
   b) eight seconds
   c) eight minutes

2. **What's the largest desert in the world?**
   a) Sahara
   b) Antarctic
   c) Great Sandy Desert

3. **Who took part in the Gunfight at the O.K. Corral?**
   a) Jesse James
   b) Billy the Kid
   c) Wyatt Earp

4. **Which character in Wonderland said "Off with their heads!":**
   the Mad Hatter **or** the Queen of Hearts?

5 The 15th century was from...
  a) 1401–1500
  b) 1500–1599
  c) 1501–1600

6 What is a thagomizer?
  a) a stegosaur's back plate
  b) the set of spikes on a stegosaur's tail
  c) a stegosaur's hoof

7 What is it called when a gas changes into a liquid?
  a) melting
  b) freezing
  c) condensation

8 Which sport did Babe Ruth
and Joe DiMaggio play?
  a) baseball
  b) basketball
  c) American football

1 Whose face "launched a thousand ships"?
a) Cleopatra   b) Helen of Troy   c) Aphrodite

2 What is the human body's biggest organ?
a) brain   b) liver   c) skin

3 New Orleans, the jazz capital of America, is also known as the 'Big...?'
a) Easy   b) Sleep   c) Apple

4 Which fictional scientist created the Monster and brought it to life with electricity:
Dr. Frankenstein **or** Dr. Jekyll?

5 During the First World War, officers sometimes received messages by homing pigeon. Could they send the pigeons back with a reply?

6 What is the lead in a pencil made from?

    a) charcoal   b) lead   c) graphite

7 Which area in the Atlantic Ocean have ships supposedly sailed into and never been seen again?

    a) The Jamaica Circle
    b) The Bermuda Triangle
    c) The Haiti Square

8 In Greek mythology, who was punished by the gods for giving mankind the secret of fire?

    a) Tantalus   b) Perseus   c) Prometheus

9 Which Roman emperor built a huge wall across northern Britain in 122 AD?

    a) Marcus Aurelius   b) Hadrian   c) Vespasian

10 What did the poet Lord Byron keep as a pet at university because dogs were not allowed?

    a) a bear   b) a parrot   c) a tiger

11 Which sport takes place in a velodrome?

    a) swimming   b) cycling   c) tennis

36

1) **Who built the Acropolis?**
   a) Romans   b) Saxons   c) Ancient Greeks

2) **Who "ate all the supper that was cooking in the saucepans":** the very hungry caterpillar **or** the tiger who came to tea?

3) **Were most dinosaurs:** plant-eaters **or** meat-eaters?

4) **Which boxer bit a chunk out of his opponent's ear?**
   a) Mike Tyson
   b) Lennox Lewis
   c) Sugar Ray Leonard

5) **What are actors often told to break before they go on stage as a message of good luck?**
   a) an arm
   b) a leg
   c) wind

6 Which character was shipwrecked on a Caribbean island?

a) Robinson Crusoe   b) Gulliver   c) Captain Ahab

7 What is the ring of water around a castle called?

a) a moat   b) a lagoon   c) a portcullis

8 Would you ever see a polar bear eating a penguin in the wild?

9 Saturn is the only planet that has rings around it. True or false?

10 Where did Charles Darwin see lots of giant tortoises?

a) Galápagos Islands   b) Barbados   c) Seychelles

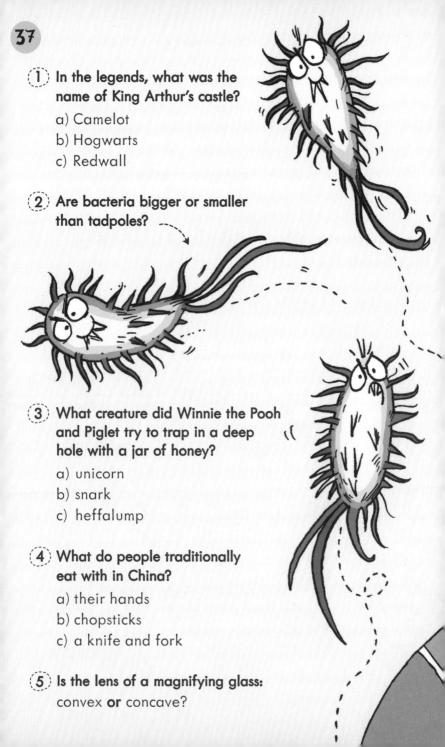

37

1. In the legends, what was the name of King Arthur's castle?
   a) Camelot
   b) Hogwarts
   c) Redwall

2. Are bacteria bigger or smaller than tadpoles?

3. What creature did Winnie the Pooh and Piglet try to trap in a deep hole with a jar of honey?
   a) unicorn
   b) snark
   c) heffalump

4. What do people traditionally eat with in China?
   a) their hands
   b) chopsticks
   c) a knife and fork

5. Is the lens of a magnifying glass: convex **or** concave?

6 What is the most popular pet worldwide?

 a) cat   b) dog   c) fish

7 Which of Doctor Who's enemies only move when you're not looking at them?

 a) The Silence   b) Weeping Angels   c) Daleks

8 What is the legendary ape that's said to walk on two legs and live in the forests of North America?

 a) Godzilla   b) King Kong   c) Bigfoot

9 I led the English Civil War against Charles I, and became the leader of the country. After I died, Charles II had my head put on a stake.

Who am I?

10 Rougly how many dust mites live in your bed?

 a) 250
 b) 2,500
 c) 25,000

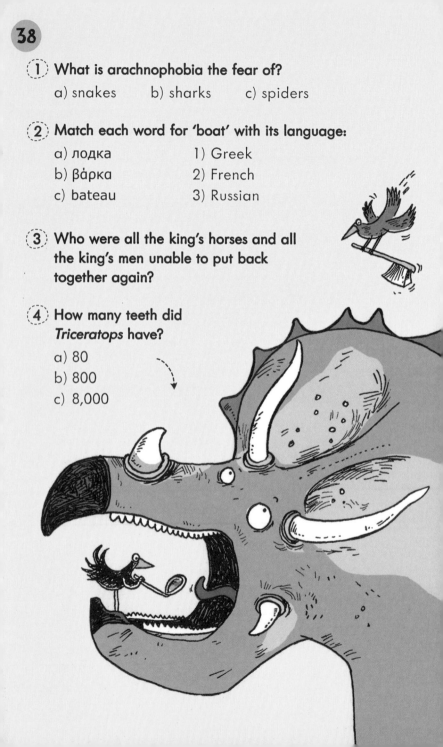

38

1. **What is arachnophobia the fear of?**
   a) snakes   b) sharks   c) spiders

2. **Match each word for 'boat' with its language:**
   a) лодка   1) Greek
   b) βάρκα   2) French
   c) bateau   3) Russian

3. **Who were all the king's horses and all the king's men unable to put back together again?**

4. **How many teeth did *Triceratops* have?**
   a) 80
   b) 800
   c) 8,000

5 How many holes are there on a standard golf course?

    a) 9   b) 14   c) 18

6 Which superhero was NOT born on Earth?

    a) Wolverine   b) Superman   c) Batman

7 In space, can anyone hear you scream?

8 Which brothers built the first ever powered aircraft:

Orville and Wilbur Wright **or** Groucho and Harpo Marx?

9 What are you supposedly given when you kiss the Blarney Stone in Ireland?

    a) the gift of the gab

    b) fabulous riches

    c) eternal youth

39

1. In *His Dark Materials*, who was friends with a warrior bear, a witch queen and the Lord of the Gyptians?

   a) Lyra   b) Hermione   c) Andromeda

2. Which Italian city is the birthplace of pizza?

   a) Naples   b) Milan   c) Rome

3. In 1871, what did the journalist Henry Morton Stanley say when he finally tracked down the explorer David Livingstone in Africa?

   a) "David, we meet at last!"
   b) "Dr. Livingstone, I presume?"
   c) "I have crossed so many, many miles to find you."

4. When knights charged at each other with wooden lances, were they: sparring **or** jousting?

5 Which television character uses the catchphrases "Ay caramba" and "Eat my shorts"?

a) Fred Flintstone b) Bart Simpson c) Scooby Doo

6 I look like a jellyfish. I float on the sea's surface. I am named after a type of old sailing ship.

What am I?

7 Where could you visit the Grand Canyon?

a) Australia b) United States c) South Africa

8 Which statement about carrots is true:
they help you see in the dark **or**
they can make you turn orange?

9 What is the moral of *The Boy Who Cried Wolf*?

a) don't lie b) don't steal c) don't cheat

10 The Ashes cricket series has been contested for over 100 years between England and which other country?

a) India b) New Zealand c) Australia

11 Which mountain was said to be the home of the Greek gods: Mount Olympus **or** Mount Sinai?

40

1. What's the name of the curtains of light that billow over Scandinavia's far north?

2. Which ingredient makes bread rise?

   a) yeast   b) flour   c) salt

3. Who marched over the Alps with elephants in his army to attack the Roman Empire?

   a) Alexander the Great
   b) Atilla the Hun
   c) Hannibal

4. What was the name of the first dog in space: Lassie **or** Laika?

(5) I fly with my umbrella. My best friend is a chimney sweep. I think a spoonful of sugar helps the medicine go down.

Who am I?

(6) What is the biggest living thing on the planet?

a) a giant redwood tree
b) a honey fungus
c) a blue whale

(7) What is the middle part of an atom called?

a) chromosome
b) nucleus
c) heart

(8) Who's the sea captain in *The Adventures of Tintin*?

a) Captain Cod
b) Captain Pollock
c) Captain Haddock

41

1. Complete the name of the ship that took the first pilgrims to America:

   The M _ _ f _ _ _ _ _

2. In the story by Jules Verne, who bet that he could fly around the world in 80 days in a hot-air balloon?

   a) Lee Scoresby   b) Phileas Fogg   c) Don Quixote

3. Which drink is best for keeping bones and teeth strong?

   a) milk   b) lemonade   c) coffee

4. I led the French army that pushed back English invaders. I was later captured and burnt at the stake. I was 19 and a woman.

   Who am I?

5. How quickly can a cheetah go from 0-60mph (0-100km/h)?

   a) 3 seconds
   b) 5 seconds
   c) 7 seconds

6) **On safari, when are you more likely to see animals drinking at a waterhole:** in the middle of the day **or** at dawn and dusk?

7) **Which cartoon character says "What's up, Doc?"**
a) Donald Duck   b) Sylvester   c) Bugs Bunny

8) **South of the Equator, water spirals down a drain in the opposite direction to north of the Equator.** True or false?

9) **Who's called the 'father of science' because he studied everything around him so closely?**
a) Aristotle
b) Plato
c) Marco Polo

42

1. **What is the nickname of the New Zealand rugby team?**
   a) All Blacks   b) Wallabies   c) Springboks

2. **Which American president was assassinated in Dallas in 1963:** Franklin D. Roosevelt **or** John F. Kennedy?

3. **What does "veni, vidi, vici" mean in English?**
   a) I'll be back
   b) Try, try, try again
   c) I came, I saw, I conquered

4. **What are the three particles that are found inside an atom?** Protons, neutrons and...
   a) gravitons   b) magnetons   c) electrons

5. **I was the terror of the seven seas. I had a long dark beard. My real name was Edward Teach, and my ship was the *Queen Anne's Revenge*. Who am I?**

6. **In *Beauty and the Beast*, why did the fairy turn the prince into a beast?**
   a) he refused her shelter from a storm
   b) he said that he wouldn't marry her
   c) he cut down her woodland home

7 What's the main obstacle to taking photos in Antarctica in mid-winter?

a) it's too cold
b) there's no light
c) it angers penguins

8 A fossil has the same shape as the original object, but is chemically more similar to what?

a) bone   b) wood   c) rock

9 In Roman gladiator shows, lions and tigers were pitted against each other. Which cat won most of the fights?

10 What did the Scarecrow ask for in *The Wizard of Oz*?

a) a brain   b) a heart   c) courage

11 Is the largest part of an iceberg: above the surface **or** below it?

12 According to her enemies, which ancient queen tested venomous snakebites on her prisoners?

a) Dido
b) Cleopatra
c) Queen of Sheba

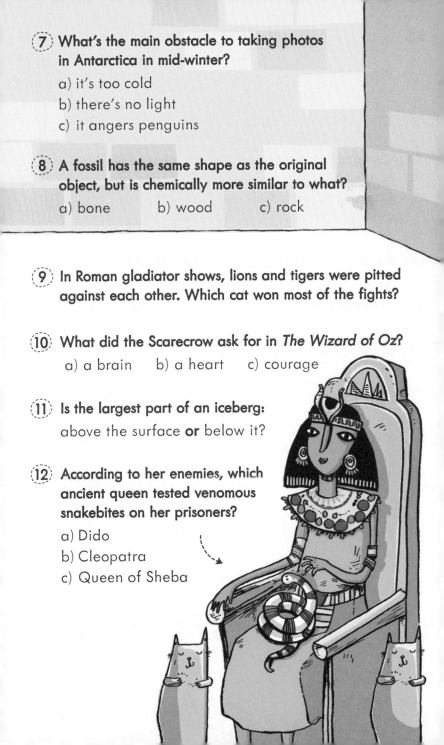

43

1. Which famous rifle is often referred to in America as 'the gun that won the west':
Winchester Model 1873 **or** Remington Model 8?

2. I have only one foot to move around on, and I have eyes on long, thin stalks. I carry my home with me on my back, wherever I go.
What am I?

3. How many degrees are there in a right angle?
   a) 90   b) 180   c) 360

4. A king in Ancient Greece wanted to know if his crown was solid gold. What did Archimedes the inventor shout when he thought of a way to test it?
   a) Bazinga!
   b) Bonanza!
   c) Eureka!

5 What is the name of the river that begins in Peru and flows through thousands of miles of dense rainforest without being crossed by a single bridge?

6 What is a horse's height measured in: feet **or** hands?

7 Who were the Japanese warriors that fought with long, curved swords?
a) samurai   b) geishas   c) jedi

8 In the story by Hans Christian Andersen, what did the ugly duckling grow up to be?
a) an ugly duck
b) a peacock
c) a swan

9 We always see the same side of the Moon in the night sky. True or false?

44

1. **Who is the founder and leader of the X-Men?**

   a) Professor Xavier   b) Nick Fury   c) Magneto

2. **Which parts of the blood attack germs:**
   white blood cells **or** red blood cells?

3. **An Antarctic research station recorded the lowest ever temperature on Earth. What was it?**

   a) −40°C (−40°F)
   b) −60°C (−75°F)
   c) −90°C (−130°F)

4. **Who was killed by an arrow in the eye at the Battle of Hastings?**

   a) William the Conqueror
   b) Edward the Confessor
   c) Harold II

5 Match each baseball team on the left to the city where that team comes from:

a) Red Sox   1) New York

b) Yankees   2) Los Angeles

c) Dodgers   3) Boston

6 Which planet is called 'the morning star' and 'the evening star' because it's seen in the sky at dawn and dusk?

a) Venus   b) Mars   c) Mercury

7 The Pharos of Alexandria was one of the Seven Wonders of the Ancient World. What was it?

a) a huge statue   b) a lighthouse   c) a library

8 Who burned down Washington D.C. in 1814?

a) Native Americans

b) the Portuguese

c) the British

9 Which of these villains is NOT one of Batman's enemies?

a) Bane   b) The Joker   c) Magneto

10 Which of these people was NOT born in Austria?

a) Mozart   b) Einstein   c) Hitler

45

1) What is said to have been hidden in the U.S. military base, Area 51?

    a) a pterosaur   b) a spy plane   c) a UFO

2) Which toy was invented in Denmark?

    a) Lego   b) yo-yo   c) Rubik's Cube

3) I am made of wood, but want to be a real boy. My nose grows every time I tell a lie. Who am I?

4) Is there more chance of something becoming a **fossil if it is:** buried quickly **or** buried slowly?

5 How did Death Valley in America get its name?

a) it's roasting hot

b) it has lots of tornadoes

c) several brutal battles were fought there

6 Which of these is NOT a real chemical element?

a) uranium   b) plutonium   c) kryptonite

7 According to legend, who led a band of outlaws called 'The Merry Men' and lived in Sherwood Forest?

a) Little John   b) Robin Hood   c) Dick Turpin

8 When squirrels store nuts for the winter, do they: bury them separately **or** bury them all in a large stash?

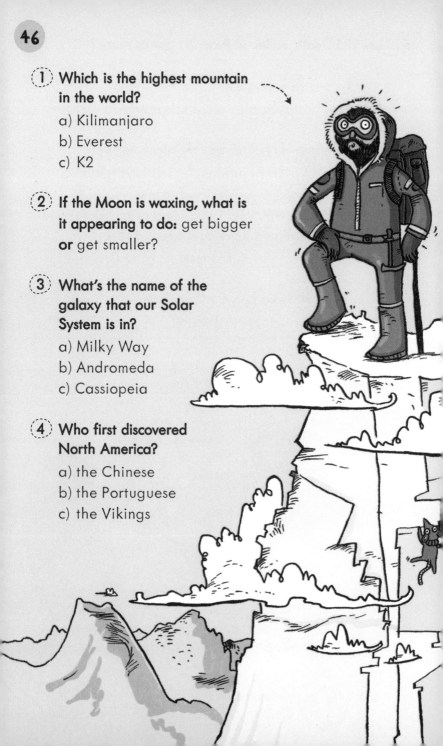

46

1. **Which is the highest mountain in the world?**
   a) Kilimanjaro
   b) Everest
   c) K2

2. **If the Moon is waxing, what is it appearing to do:** get bigger **or** get smaller?

3. **What's the name of the galaxy that our Solar System is in?**
   a) Milky Way
   b) Andromeda
   c) Cassiopeia

4. **Who first discovered North America?**
   a) the Chinese
   b) the Portuguese
   c) the Vikings

5 **What is Scrooge's first name in *A Christmas Carol*?**
   a) Ebenezer   b) Severus   c) Uriah

6 **Which of these is NOT a horse race?**
   a) Grand National
   b) Kentucky Derby
   c) Dakar Rally

7 **What is the record age for a giant tortoise?**
   a) 55 years   b) 155 years   c) 255 years

8 **Which gladiator escaped captivity and led a revolt against the Romans:** Maximus **or** Spartacus?

9 **Who was the pharaoh inside this coffin?**
   a) Tutankhamun
   b) Rameses II
   c) Ptolemy I

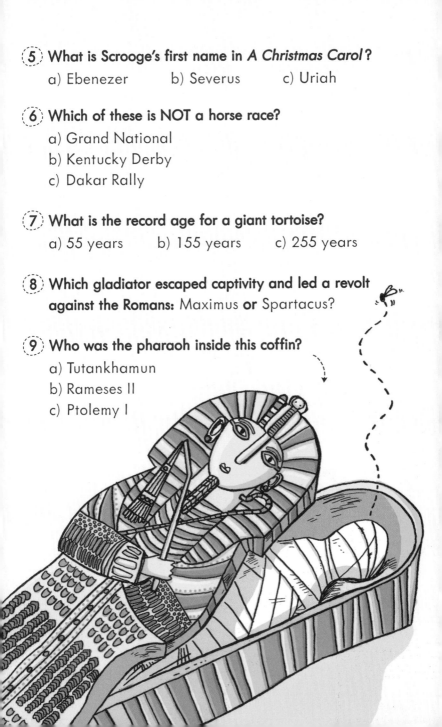

47

1. I wore a white shawl and sandals, and led my country's revolution against the British. I told my followers not to use violence, but was shot by my enemies.

   Who am I?

2. In the *Harry Potter* books, which type of dragon did Rubeus Hagrid hatch in his fire:

   Hungarian Horntail **or** Norwegian Ridgeback?

3. Which country's international team has won the FIFA World Cup the most times?

   a) Germany   b) Brazil   c) Italy

4. Who is this famous scientist?

5 Which fictional bear was found in a train station and has a particular liking for English marmalade?

a) Winnie the Pooh   b) Baloo   c) Paddington

6 If you see an oasis in the desert that disappears as you walk toward it, what have you actually seen?

A m _ _ _ _ _

7 Which seahorses give birth: male **or** female?

8 What was the name of the Muslim leader who drove the Christian crusaders out of Jerusalem?

a) Aladdin   b) Saladin   c) Paladin

9 Who was the first person to 'split the atom':
J. Robert Oppenheimer **or** Ernest Rutherford?

1. Which of these animals were NOT around at the same time as the dinosaurs?

   a) crocodiles   b) sharks   c) woolly mammoths

2. In the fairy tale, what did Cinderella leave behind at the ball: a glass slipper **or** a ruby slipper?

3. Which legendary land is said to have been lost underwater?

   a) Asgard   b) Atlantis   c) Avalon

4. What is amber?

   a) fossilized tree resin
   b) molten rock in a volcano
   c) a spicy tomato sauce

5. In early Victorian times, chimney sweeps started work at what age?

   a) 6   b) 12   c) 18

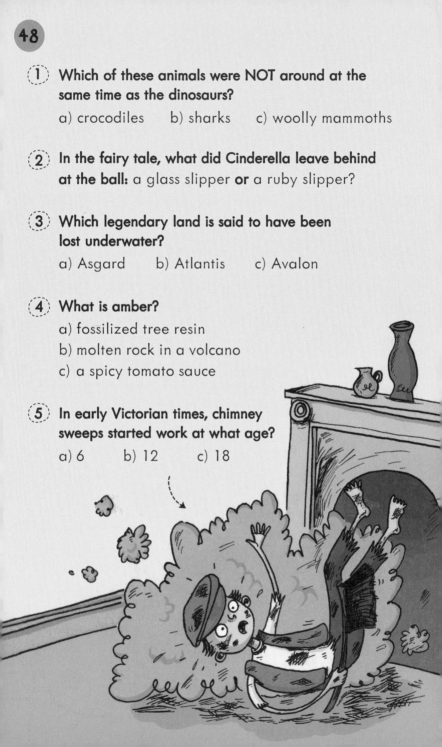

6. I used to live alone in my swamp... until Lord Farquaad forced me to rescue Princess Fiona from a dragon. My best friend is a talking donkey.
Who am I?

7. Which ship was found mysteriously abandoned and drifting in the ocean, with no sign of damage and no sign of her crew?
   a) *Santa María*   b) *Mary Celeste*   c) *Cutty Sark*

8. What was the name of the panther in *The Jungle Book*?
   a) Shere Khan   b) Akela   c) Bagheera

9. In which sport might you score with a slam dunk, a layup, or a free throw?
   a) basketball   b) quidditch   c) water polo

10. Koalas are a type of bear. True or false?

11. What was on the island of Alcatraz?
    a) monastery
    b) military hospital
    c) maximum-security prison

12. Copenhagen, in Denmark, has a statue of which fairy-tale character looking out over the sea?
    a) ugly duckling   b) little mermaid   c) snow maiden

1. What is the name for a group of small islands?
   a) archipelago
   b) estuary
   c) lagoon

2. Who were the Viking warriors with the most fearsome reputation for bloodlust: berserkers **or** valkyries?

3. Match the correct name with each superhero:
   a) Bruce Wayne   1) Spiderman
   b) Tony Stark   2) Batman
   c) Peter Parker   3) Iron Man

4. What was Florence Nightingale's nickname?
   a) The Angel of the Crimea
   b) The Lady with the Lamp
   c) The Soldiers' Saint

DWWWWW!

5. Which animal has the most powerful bite in the world?

a) tiger shark   b) crocodile   c) lion

6. What underground demon almost killed Gandalf in *The Lord of the Rings*?

a) Shelob   b) Smaug   c) the Balrog

7. I love crackers and cheese and cups of tea. I've been attacked by a criminal penguin and a robotic dog. I have a friend named Gromit. Who am I?

8. What were humans using first: fire or the wheel?

1. **What did the Ancient Greeks do calculations on?**
   a) an abacus   b) a calculator   c) a computer

2. **Which is the closest star to the Earth?**

3. **Which plane defended Britain from invasion in the Second World War?**
   a) Messerschmitt 109   b) Spitfire   c) MiG-1

4. **Who's said to live in a snowy place called Lapland, in the Arctic Circle?**
   a) White Queen   b) Santa Claus   c) Snow Maiden

5. **What's the name for a group of sharks:**
   a shudder **or** a shiver?

6 What did Hansel and Gretel come across in the woods?

 a) a big, bad wolf
 b) a family of fairies
 c) a gingerbread house

7 Who was the first person to fly solo across the Atlantic:

 Charles Lindbergh **or** Louis Blériot?

8 The flat-topped mountain that overlooks Cape Town in South Africa is called what?

 a) Footrest Mountain
 b) Table Mountain
 c) Pedestal Mountain

9 In the *Asterix* comic books, what does Obelix like to eat most of all?

 a) wild boar   b) chicken legs   c) roast beef

10 Bats hunt at night using...

 a) moonlight   b) smells   c) echoes

11 During which war did the Light Brigade make a heroic cavalry charge against heavy artillery:

 the Crimean War **or** the Vietnam War?

12 In the comic books inspired by Norse mythology, what is the name of Thor's adopted brother?

 a) Fandral   b) Odin   c) Loki

1. Antibiotics help your body fight viruses.
   True or false?

2. What is the movie hero Jack Sparrow?
   a) vampire hunter   b) archaeologist   c) pirate

3. Which beetle did the Ancient Egyptians worship?
   a) goliath beetle   b) scarab beetle   c) stag beetle

4. What was the U.S. naval base that was attacked by
   Japanese pilots during the Second World War?
   a) Gold Harbor
   b) Pearl Harbor
   c) Sapphire Harbor

5. Which African animal is nicknamed
   'the laughing assassin'?
   a) hyena   b) crocodile   c) giraffe

6. What is glass made from?
   a) salt   b) wood   c) sand

7. Where is the Great Barrier Reef?
   a) Australia   b) Madagascar   c) India

8 In *Three Billy Goats Gruff*, what sort of creature was living under the bridge?

a) goblin   b) sphinx   c) troll

9 What is the name for the long, thin loaf of bread that is often seen as a symbol of France?

a) naan   b) baguette   c) ciabatta

10 Which city's people were tricked into taking this hollow horse, packed full of Greek soldiers, inside their walls?

a) Rome   b) Sparta   c) Troy

Answers

1 **1.** gold, silver and bronze **2.** snozzcumbers **3.** b **4.** c **5.** lightning (A lightning strike increases the temperature and pressure of the air. This makes it expand very rapidly, creating the sound we call thunder.) **6.** b **7.** a **8.** c **9.** false (it was fought between England and France from 1337 to 1453, actually lasting 116 years)

2 **1.** b **2.** ice **3.** c **4.** a **5.** playing possum **6.** c (its first manned flight was in 1783) **7.** a **8.** white **9.** no (apples didn't evolve until after dinosaurs had become extinct) **10.** b

3 **1.** b **2.** no, they are meteors (small bits of space rock, burning up as they enter Earth's atmosphere) **3.** Ayers Rock **4.** a **5.** Nelson Mandela (he was president of South Africa from 1994 to 1999) **6.** b **7.** b **8.** c (in *The Lion, the Witch and the Wardrobe*) **9.** a

4 **1.** a **2.** c (in the bone marrow) **3.** c **4.** b **5.** *Treasure Island*, by Robert Louis Stevenson **6.** c **7.** b (it's easily deep enough to submerge Mount Everest, which stands at 29,026ft. (8,848m)) **8.** b **9.** St. George **10.** a

5 **1.** b **2.** c **3.** a (he was the Pied Piper of Hamelin, which is in Lower Saxony) **4.** c **5.** Great Wall of China **6.** b **7.** c (Montreal is a mainly French-speaking city) **8.** b

6 **1.** the Grinch (in the poem by Dr. Seuss) **2.** c **3.** b **4.** false (slow worms are legless lizards) **5.** a (The Great Red Spot, which is a huge storm, is large enough to contain two or three planets the size of the Earth.) **6.** an owl **7.** c **8.** b **9.** the Jolly Roger **10.** a

7 **1.** Muhammad Ali **2.** karate **3.** b (African bush, African forest, and Asian) **4.** Ned Kelly **5.** c **6.** a (it's in Venezuela) **7.** c **8.** a

 8 **1.** b **2.** c **3.** a **4.** b **5.** a2, b1 (the male calls tu-whoo, the female calls tu-whit) **6.** true **7.** a (because it was extremely uncomfortable to ride) **8.** no (snakes don't have ears) **9.** the Gruffalo

 9 **1.** c **2.** right **3.** b (red was the House of Lancaster, white was the House of York) **4.** c (they stand up to look out for them) **5.** b **6.** a (it's called the TARDIS, which stands for Time and Relative Dimension in Space) **7.** b **8.** c **9.** a murder

10 **1.** sirens **2.** a **3.** Atlas **4.** b **5.** b (d'Artagnan was the young man who wanted to join the musketeers; Richelieu was the conspiring cardinal) **6.** b **7.** a **8.** c **9.** b

11 **1.** a **2.** b (a sting from a box jellyfish can kill a human in two minutes) **3.** b **4.** c **5.** an insulator **6.** c **7.** a **8.** c

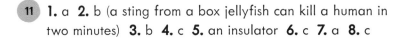 **12** **1.** b **2.** c **3.** false **4.** a **5.** b **6.** sunflowers **7.** Genghis Khan **8.** b

13 **1.** a **2.** c **3.** c **4.** leeches (in the Middle Ages, medics believed many illnesses could be cured by draining blood, so they often used blood-sucking leeches in their treatments) **5.** b **6.** a **7.** c **8.** c

14 **1.** b **2.** c **3.** b **4.** yes **5.** a **6.** b **7.** Solar eclipse **8.** b **9.** Achilles (Hence the expression 'Achilles' heel'. The story goes that his mother tried to make him immortal by dipping him in the River Styx as a baby, but the heel she held him by did not enter the water.) **10.** c (it carries deadly diseases) **11.** c

15 **1.** c **2.** Antoni Gaudí **3.** b **4.** Tasmanian Devil **5.** a **6.** b **7.** a **8.** a2, b3, c1

16 **1.** c (there isn't any water on the Moon's surface, but early astronomers mistook the Moon's darker patches for seas, hence the names) **2.** true (it's short for deoxyribonucleic acid) **3.** c **4.** Tiger (spelled 'Tyger' in the poem) **5.** b **6.** nine days **7.** Teenage Mutant Ninja Turtles **8.** b **9.** Roald Amundsen (Roald Dahl was named after him) **10.** a

17 **1.** a **2.** b **3.** b **4.** Venus (although Mercury is closer to the Sun, Venus's dense atmosphere means it is far hotter) **5.** c (seven) **6.** Mario **7.** a **8.** b **9.** c (there's one for each state)

18 **1.** b (although Russia is larger, Canada's coastline is longer because it has so many islands) **2.** true **3.** c (they are roughly the same size so the air resistance would be virtually the same, and gravity exerts the same force on all objects, regardless of their mass) **4.** c **5.** b **6.** horror frog **7.** false (they are white, and only turn pink later because of all the shrimp they eat) **8.** *Titanic* **9.** c (The name comes from the legend of Pheidippides, a Greek messenger who was said to have run straight from the Battle of Marathon (490 BC) to Athens with the message that they had defeated the Persians, covering roughly the distance of a modern marathon.) **10.** b

19 **1.** b **2.** c (in the poem by Edward Lear) **3.** a **4.** a **5.** a
6. yes (they are capable of producing shocks of up to
860 volts) **7.** c **8.** Heracles (which is the Greek name for
Hercules) **9.** black with white stripes (the white stripes are
areas where the fur's natural pigmentation is absent)

20 **1.** true (Although occasionally tiny snow crystals fall from
the sky. These haven't grown into snowflakes, and look
very similar to each other.) **2.** b (as they were preparing
to face the Spanish Armada) **3.** a **4.** Komodo dragon
5. killer whale (they are much bigger and more intelligent)
6. c **7.** Ferdinand Magellan (he died in the Philippines in
1521, about two thirds of the way through his 'round the
world' voyage) **8.** b **9.** b **10.** c (it was originally a Dutch
settlement, but was renamed after the Duke of York when
English forces seized control of it)

21 **1.** b **2.** b **3.** c **4.** shoot it with a silver bullet **5.** c **6.** b
(he was from the former Soviet Union, and blasted into
space on April 12, 1961) **7.** false (Eskimo has about the
same number of words for snow as English. But the Sami
people, who live in the far North of the Nordic countries,
have about 300 words for snow.) **8.** James Bond **9.** a
10. a

22 **1.** b **2.** c **3.** b, c, a **4.** black hole **5.** c **6.** a **7.** c
8. 'The Greatest Show on Earth' **9.** b

23 **1.** c **2.** b **3.** northwest **4.** gondola **5.** mercury **6.** c
7. a **8.** a

24 1. b 2. yes (a passenger jet is struck by lightning about once a year, but is designed to withstand the strike) 3. b 4. a 5. c (many are killed for shark fin soup; others get caught up in fishing nets) 6. waterfall (It is the locals' name for Victoria Falls in Africa. Although it is neither the highest nor the widest, it is the largest single sheet of falling water in the world.) 7. b, d, c, a 8. a 9. c

25 1. b (scurvy is caused by a lack of vitamin c, and lemons contain a lot of it) 2. a 3. b 4. the midnight sun (from late May to late July, the Sun never completely sets there) 5. b (Saltwater freezes at a lower temperature than fresh water. The salt dissolves into the ice, lowering its melting point.) 6. b (it's so fast, it inspired a form of martial art) 7. a 8. Tarzan 9. c 10. false (the line was in use long before Marie Antoinette, and there is no evidence she ever said it)

26 1. a 2. a (they are so tiny that they would all fit on your thumbnail) 3. c 4. "E.T. phone home" 5. b 6. b 7. c 8. Sleeping Beauty 9. b 10. c 11. a 12. false (And anyway, there's no point. Once they've gone past halfway, they might as well have set out in the opposite direction.) 13. a

27 1. a 2. tragedy 3. b 4. c 5. a (in the book of the same name by Herman Melville) 6. nine 7. b 8. a 9. c

28 1. a 2. c 3. a (a triangle is an international distress symbol) 4. a 5. b 6. a 7. a 8. c 9. b 10. c 11. exothermic

29 1. b (they're the same units that boat speed is measured in) 2. a2, b1 3. c 4. a 5. b 6. the Bastille 7. c 8. a 9. b (in *James and the Giant Peach* by Roald Dahl) 10. c 11. b (rhinos have poor vision, and follow their ears more than their eyes)

30 1. true 2. General Custer 3. a 4. c 5. yes (all living things have DNA) 6. back one day (On a map of the world, time goes forward as you move eastward. At the furthest point east, you reach the International Date Line. You are 24 hours ahead of the furthest point west, but because the Earth is round, if you take one more step, you go back 24 hours.) 7. no 8. a 9. b 10. a

31 1. b 2. c (air resistance means that it would fall slowly) 3. Sherlock Holmes 4. South Pole 5. William Shakespeare 6. false (You'd swell up slightly, but you wouldn't explode, or freeze, and your blood wouldn't boil. You'd pass out after 30 seconds from lack of oxygen, and after that you'd die.) 7. a (the 'scream' is air escaping from the shell) 8. a 9. c 10. b 11. c

32 1. c 2. no (they are the largest member of the dolphin family) 3. a 4. b 5. c 6. dynamite 7. b 8. Vikings

33 1. c 2. a 3. b 4. a 5. c 6. false 7. b 8. c 9. a

34 1. c 2. b (a desert is somewhere where it hardly ever rains or snows, and Antarctica is the most cloudless place on Earth) 3. c 4. the Queen of Hearts 5. a 6. b 7. c 8. a

35 1. b (the quotation, spelled 'launch'd', is from Christopher Marlowe's play *Doctor Faustus*) 2. c 3. a 4. Dr. Frankenstein 5. no (they only fly in one direction – home) 6. c 7. b 8. c 9. b 10. a 11. b

36 1. c 2. the tiger who came to tea 3. plant-eaters 4. a 5. b 6. a (in the book by Daniel Defoe) 7. a 8. no (polar bears live near the North Pole; penguins live near the South Pole) 9. false (Jupiter, Uranus and Neptune have rings too) 10. a

37 1. a 2. smaller 3. c 4. b 5. convex 6. a (cats are more adaptable than dogs because they don't need as much attention or space) 7. b 8. c 9. Oliver Cromwell 10. c

38 1. c 2. a3, b1, c2 3. Humpty Dumpty 4. b 5. c 6. b 7. no (there are no air particles in space to carry the sound) 8. Orville and Wilbur Wright (it was called the *Wright Flyer*, and its first flight was in 1903) 9. a

39 1. a 2. a 3. b 4. jousting 5. b 6. Portuguese man o' war 7. b 8. they can make you turn orange (the myth about carrots helping you see in the dark was spread by British intelligence in the Second World War because they didn't want Germany to know that they'd invented a radar system) 9. a 10. c 11. Mount Olympus

40 1. Northern Lights (they are also known as the Aurora Borealis) 2. a 3. c 4. Laika 5. Mary Poppins 6. b (It lives in Oregon, USA, and is mostly underground. It covers 9km² (3.5sq. miles) and is at least 2,400 years old.) 7. b 8. c

41 1. The Mayflower 2. b (in *Around the World in 80 Days*) 3. a 4. Joan of Arc 5. a (it can reach 70mph (110km/h) 6. at dawn and dusk (when it's cooler) 7. c 8. false (anywhere in the world, water can spiral down a drain in either direction) 9. a

42 1. a 2. John F. Kennedy 3. c 4. c 5. Blackbeard 6. a 7. b (at the Poles in winter, the Sun never rises) 8. c 9. tigers 10. a 11. below it (icebergs are floating in the sea; only the top part sticks out above the water) 12. b

43 1. Winchester Model 1873 2. a snail 3. a 4. c 5. Amazon
6. hands 7. a 8. c 9. true

44 1. a 2. white blood cells 3. c (it was recorded in 1983 at
a Russian station called Vostok) 4. c 5. a3, b1, c2 6. a
7. b 8. c 9. c 10. b (Einstein was born in Germany)

45 1. c (it's said to have crash-landed in Roswell, New
Mexico, and been taken to Area 51 in Nevada) 2. a
3. Pinocchio 4. buried quickly (there's less chance of it
being eaten or decaying before it can become preserved)
5. a (It's the world's hottest desert. Its record temperature
is 56.7°C (134°F).) 6. c (there is an element called
krypton, but kryptonite is a fictional mineral that comes
from Superman's home planet and drains his strength)
7. b 8. bury them separately

46 1. b 2. get bigger (when it appears to be getting smaller,
it is waning) 3. a 4. c 5. a 6. c 7. c 8. Spartacus 9. a
(he was pharaoh of Ancient Egypt from 1332-1323 BC,
and his tomb was discovered in the Valley of the Kings by
Howard Carter in 1922)

47 1. Mahatma Gandhi 2. Norwegian Ridgeback 3. b
(five times) 4. Albert Einstein (he is famous for his wild,
white hair, and for the equation $E = mc^2$) 5. c (he was
named after the station he was found in) 6. a mirage
7. male 8. b 9. Ernest Rutherford

48 1. c 2. a glass slipper 3. b 4. a 5. a 6. Shrek 7. b 8. c
9. a 10. false 11. c 12. b

49 **1.** a **2.** berserkers (This is where the word 'berserk' comes from. Valkyries were female figures who were said to choose who lived and who died in battle.) **3.** a2, b3, c1 **4.** b **5.** b **6.** c **7.** Wallace **8.** fire

50 **1.** a **2.** the Sun **3.** b **4.** b **5.** a shiver **6.** c **7.** Charles Lindbergh (in 1927, he flew from New York to Paris in his plane *Spirit of St. Louis*, taking 33 and a half hours to complete the journey) **8.** b **9.** a **10.** c **11.** the Crimean War **12.** c

51 **1.** false (antibiotics help your body fight bacterial infections, but not viruses) **2.** c (in the *Pirates of the Caribbean* movies) **3.** b **4.** b (it's in Hawaii, and was attacked on December 7th, 1941) **5.** a (its call sounds like snatches of hysterical laughter) **6.** c **7.** a **8.** c **9.** b **10.** c (According to Homer, the Greeks pretended to have abandoned their attack on Troy, leaving the giant wooden horse as a parting gift. Once it was taken inside the city walls and the Trojans were off their guard, the soldiers inside snuck out and opened the gates for the rest of the Greek army to capture and destroy the city.)

With thanks to Michael Hill

First published in 2015 by Usborne Publishing Ltd, 83–85 Saffron Hill, London ECIN 8RT, England.